DIAMO TEARS

Stories for Assembly

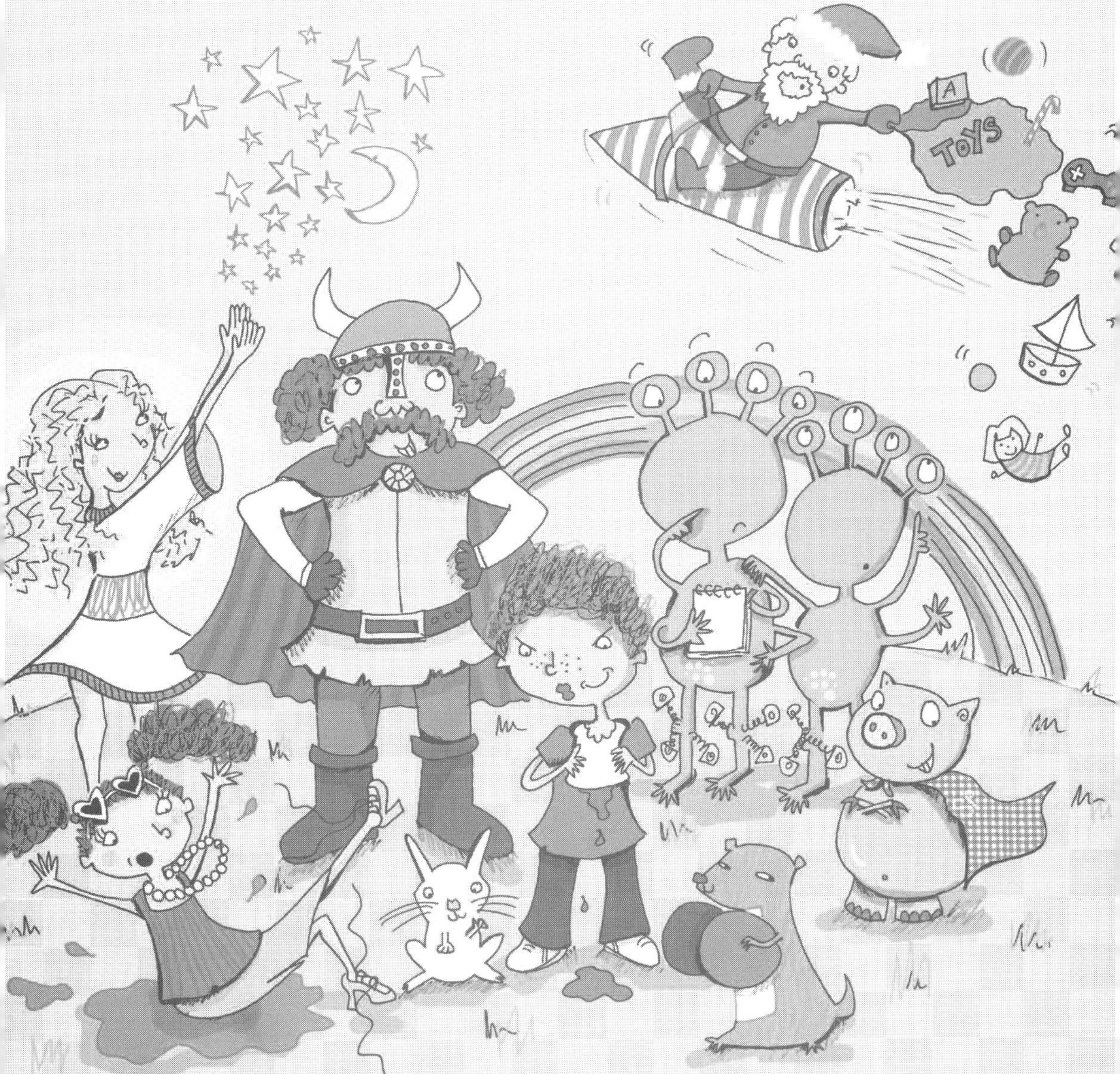

Caroline Picking and **Edward Preston**

CDs

There are two CDs; one contains the lyrics and scores and the other, the music.

Each story in the book is accompanied by a song which can be used in the assembly. On the CDs you'll find the relevant score, music and photocopiable lyrics. In the case of the Harvest there is also some dance music, (The Grasshopper's Cumbia), that you may wish to incorporate in the assembly.

Copyright Music and Text © Caroline Picking and Edward Preston, 2010
Copyright © Illustrations Clare Elsom
First published 2010 by Southgate Publishers Ltd

Southgate Publishers Ltd, The Square, Sandford, Crediton, Devon EX17 4LW
All rights reserved. No part of this publication may be reproduced, copied or transmitted in any form or by any means, electronic, mechanical, photocopying, recording or otherwise, without the prior written permission of the publisher or in accordance with the Copyright, Design and Patents Act 1988.

Printed and bound in Great Britain by Short Run Press, Exeter, UK.
British Library Cataloguing in Publication Data
A CIP catalogue record for this book is available from the British Library.

ISBN 9781857 411676

Acknowledgements
Jonathan Gower, Sandford Primary School

Contents

1. The Brave Little Pigs — 5
Being brave; supporting each other gives courage

2. Llewellyn and his Dog — 9
Being hot-headed and impulsive; jumping to conclusions and having to live with the consequences

3. Diamond Tears — 12
Greed; the value of happiness

4. King Canute — 15
Taking responsibility

5. The Big Lion and the Little Rabbit — 18
Stand up to bullies

6. Olga at Sports Day — 22
Pressures of consumerism; the importance of owning the 'right' labels; peer pressure

7. Santa in a Muddle — 25
Coping with changes

8. Springtime – the Joy of Nature's Creation — 28
Creation myths; caring for our world; the joy of spring

9. Harvest — 31
A time to work hard; share; think of others and be thankful for what we have

10. Differences — 34
Be tolerant; don't judge by appearances; embrace differences; don't prejudge others

11. Mother's Day — 37
Our mothers are special

12. Tanabata – a Japanese Festival — 41
Work hard to achieve goals; loyalty; tenacity

13. Visitors from Outer Space — 44
Welcoming visitors; following school rules; being part of a caring community

Introduction

This book and CD package aims to provide everything you need for school assemblies, suitable for use with KS2 children. The stories are a combination of traditional folk tales, fables from around the world and fresh new stories, all focusing on a different theme.

Questions to stimulate reflection and interaction are provided, as well as optional prayers to close the assembly. Links with the Bible are suggested, to encourage further exploration of the themes from a Christian viewpoint. Additionally, further links with literature, poetry, films and books are given. These can be used to develop a topic or to relate an idea more widely. Quotes from a range of sources are given; often, these can provide an opening and a focus to an assembly. Suggestions for further activities are also provided under the heading: "You could also." These ideas link the assemblies to areas of curriculum study.

A CD featuring backing tracks for songs to accompany each assembly can be used by specialists and non-specialists alike; easy piano arrangements and lyric sheets are also provided.

1. The Brave Little Pigs

> Being brave; supporting each other gives courage

Deep in the forest in a small brick house lived three, kind little pigs. They always thought about others and helped whenever they could. For example, whenever Old Mother Hubbard's dog was howling with hunger, they would rush round to her house with a juicy bone. Everyone knew how thoughtful they were.

But one day, the biggest little pig received a call on his mobile. It was from Red Riding Hood. She was going to stay at the castle until midnight, helping Cinderella to clear up after a party. She had a favour to ask the little pigs. She wanted them to take some porridge to her grandma's. Poor Grandma had a visit from Goldilocks yesterday and the greedy girl had scoffed all her porridge, so she was feeling rather peckish.

"Of course we'll help! Let's go!" cried the biggest little pig, pulling on his 'SUPERPIG' cape.

But the other little pigs were terrified. They hadn't forgotten what had happened to their cousins long ago. The Big Bad Wolf had paid them a visit and huffed and puffed until their houses were blown down.

"I'm scared! The Big Bad Wolf might be waiting on the roof of Grandma's cottage. I don't want to be a sausage roll!"

The biggest little pig took the smallest little pig by the trotter. He reminded her that the Big Bad Wolf had been cooked in a pot when he climbed down the chimney, so he wouldn't be able to catch any more pigs. Also, he reminded her about poor Grandma.

"What about Grandma? She'll be starving if we don't take her this porridge! If we stay on the paths as our parents told us, we'll be safe."

This made the smallest little pig think. She decided she must be brave and do what is right. After all, a wolf stew was nothing to be worried about!

As they set off, the middle little pig suddenly remembered what had nearly happened to Grandma last year.

"I'm scared! The other Big Bad Wolf might be dressed up as Grandma inside her cottage. I don't want to be a bacon sandwich!"

The biggest little pig took the middle little pig by the trotter. He reminded him that the other Big Bad Wolf had been chased away by the woodcutter, so he wouldn't be able to catch any more pigs. Also, he reminded him about poor Grandma.

"What about Grandma? She'll be starving if we don't take her this porridge! If we stay on the paths as our parents told us, we'll be safe."

This made the middle little pig think. He decided that if his brother and sister were with him, he would feel much stronger and able to face any fears. Also, he knew that Grandma needed her porridge and he really wanted to help.

As the three little pigs walked through the deep, dark forest they heard lots of worrying noises. They listened as the Billy Goats Gruff sang a spooky song about trolls... but then they remembered they were just three silly kids who were always trying to scare each other. They heard a strange whistling sound coming from under the ground... but then they remembered the seven dwarfs were working in the mine below them. And when they saw an old lady with a shiny red apple in a basket coming towards them, they remembered the advice their parents had given them to never speak to strangers, so they just walked right past.

At last they got to Grandma's cottage. They'd done it! They felt very brave and very pleased with themselves. Grandma was sitting up in bed waiting for them. All the little pigs gasped when she smiled.

"Grandma! What big teeth you have!"

But they needn't have worried. Grandma had been to the dentist that morning and now she had a nice new set of false teeth – all the better to eat porridge with.

Reflection

Every day we may face new challenges.
Think quietly for a minute about a challenge you've worried about this week.
Maybe:
"How can I make up with my friend?"
"Should I do what my neighbour is telling me to do?"
Did you do the right thing? Can you change what you did?

We should try to be brave and make the right choices.
When we tackle new challenges we can feel pleased with ourselves for doing the right thing. Think about a time you've been brave recently. Maybe:
"I didn't join in with teasing."
"I stood up to a bully."
Give yourself a pat on the back for being brave.
We feel stronger when our friends are there to help us.
Let's be a good friend to others and give them courage to make difficult decisions.

Links

Harry Potter stories by J.K. Rowling Harry and his friends stand up to Voldermort.
The Wizard of Oz The Cowardly Lion searched for courage ("You're right – I haven't any courage! I even scare myself!").

Bible links

Esther 2-8 Jews tell the story of Esther's bravery to remind themselves that God is with them in every situation.

Quote

"An army of sheep led by a lion would defeat an army of lions led by a sheep." Arab proverb

Prayer

Response: "We will be brave."

Lord,
When we are faced with fear – Response
When our work seems too hard and we want to give up – Response
When someone else looks to us to provide the lead – Response
When we see bullying and we are afraid to step in – Response
When others mock us for doing the right thing – Response
We know you are there beside us, giving us the strength to carry on – Response
Amen.

You could also:
- Write new endings for traditional fairy tales to include aspects of bravery.
- Carry out a whole school survey on how pupils travel to school, using graphs to present the results.
- Discuss scenarios and strategies for guarding against stranger danger.
- Invent a board game. Make a track from Home to Grandma's, featuring hazards such as Troll's Bridge, Wolf's Lair and so on; three pig playing pieces from clay; a spinner for a die and some forfeit cards to highlight the dangers of the journey such as: 'Spot Troll in the distance. Run back home to safety.'

2. Llewellyn and his Dog

> Being hot-headed and impulsive; jumping to conclusions and having to live with the consequences

Prince Llewellyn was a fine huntsman and all the men in Wales admired his skill. He often rode through the forests chasing deer or rabbits, proudly returning to his castle with meat for his servants to prepare for supper. He was young and fit, but hot-headed and quick to lose his temper. Still, this fierce nature meant he was an excellent fighter, so all his men respected him.

Llewellyn had a magnificent hunting dog – a smooth, sleek greyhound named Gellert. Gellert was swifter than forked lightning, sharp and bright, tearing through the forests at his master's command, outwitting rabbits and outrunning hares. He was intelligent and obedient, always crouching at Llewellyn's feet, watching and waiting for the signal to do his duty. The enormous animal was never far from his master's side, even sleeping by his bed in the castle every night. One ear, however, was always cocked, listening for danger. The prince loved Gellert deeply and he knew the animal would do anything to protect him.

However, there was someone whom Llewellyn loved even more – his baby son. The child was the light of his life – a happy, smiling baby with dark brown hair and chubby little fists. He lay in his cradle contentedly, sleeping, cooing or playing with his toes. Each night, Llewellyn stroked the sleeping child's soft, smooth face and listened to the sound of his gentle breathing as he slumbered. "Nothing shall ever hurt you," he whispered in the baby's ear. "I shall make certain of that." Then he wrapped his rabbit-skin rug carefully around him and headed out into the dark to hunt with his dogs.

One bitterly cold night, Prince Llewellyn mounted his horse and waited impatiently outside his castle. The animal stamped the ground restlessly and whinnied as his master blew on his hunting horn – the signal for the dogs to follow. But although the others came, Llewellyn's favourite dog, Gellert, was nowhere to be seen. Angrily, the prince sounded the horn again but still the big greyhound did not appear. Fat snowflakes had begun to twirl out of the sky, so the hunting party could waste no more time. Finally Llewellyn set off in a furious temper towards the forest. How dare Gellert disobey him! There'd be no treats for him that night!

Three exhausting hours later, Llewellyn and his animals returned to the castle. The snow was falling even faster now and, worse, they hadn't caught a single thing – it had been too hard to see. The prince was even angrier than he had been earlier.

Then, as he swept into his chambers in the castle, a terrible sight greeted him. The baby's cradle was flung upside-down on the floor and his blankets were strewn around the room. The rabbit-skin rug was chewed and torn and lying in a heap on top of the cradle. Llewellyn called out for his son but there was no reply. As he gasped with horror, he saw Gellert emerging from behind the door. The dog's jaws were covered in blood and he was panting heavily. A shred of the baby's nightgown was caught between his giant teeth. It was clear he had been in a savage fight to the death. Llewellyn scanned the room frantically but there was no sign of the child. Wild with grief, the prince cried out: "My son! You've killed my son!" Grabbing his sword, he rounded on Gellert and thrust it into the dog's side. With a shudder, the animal fell to the floor. He was quite, quite dead.

And then, from beneath the cradle, there came a sound. Llewellyn stumbled to his feet and, in a daze, staggered round to where the noise was coming from. To his amazement, under the cot lay his son, alive under the covers and protected by the bars of the cradle. Horrified, the prince scooped up the child in his arms What had happened? Slowly, he looked around and suddenly saw the body of a large, grey wolf lying behind the door, his throat savaged. He too was quite, quite dead. Crouching over the body of his faithful dog, Llewellyn wept pitifully, for now he realised that the brave dog had rescued the child by killing the wolf just as the creature had tried to attack him! "Dearest Gellert," he sobbed, "you protected my child and killed the wolf who threatened him, but now I have killed you. I should have trusted you and known you would always be faithful. I was too quick to judge, and now I shall pay for that moment of anger for ever."

But Llewellyn could never change what he had done. If only he had not been so hot-headed and quick to believe his friend had let him down.

Prince Llewellyn built a monument to Gellert at the foot of Mount Snowdon. It is called Bedgellert, and you can still visit it today.

Reflection

What words could you use to describe Gellert the dog?
What about Llewellyn?
What did Llewellyn think Gellert had done?
What had really happened?
Have you ever 'jumped to the wrong conclusion' about somebody or about their behaviour?

What makes someone a trusted friend?
Llewellyn tried to make up for his terrible mistake by building a memorial to Gellert. How can you make up when you make a mistake and upset a friend?

Links

The Brahman and the Mongoose (from the Panchatantra)
This tale from India tells how a woman killed a mongoose which she believed had attacked her child. In her haste she did not realise the mongoose had, in fact, protected the baby from a cobra.
King Lear by William Shakespeare
King Lear acted in haste and banished the wrong daughter.

Bible links

Exodus 2 11-15. Impetuous Moses kills the Egyptian.

Quote

"What you don't see with your eyes, don't witness with your mouth."
Jewish proverb

Prayer

Lord,
Sometimes we don't see the good in others.
Help us to value the good in others every day.
When we are judgmental, let us pause to consider.
Sometimes we are quick to anger.
When we feel anger, let us be calm.
Sometimes we treat others unfairly.
When we are thoughtless, let us make amends.
Amen.

You could also:
- Play Chinese whispers in Circle Time – saying nice things about others.
- Have a 'Star of the Week' for each pupil in turn – make a certificate, describing all their best characteristics.
- Write an acrostic poem about a friend.

3. Diamond Tears

> Greed; the value of happiness

Far, far away from here, on a hillside, lived an old man. He had a small but comfortable house with a garden full of pretty wild flowers, a kind wife and two pets – a sleepy old cat and a puppy. A stream ran by his house where he could catch fish for supper, and there were fruit trees nearby where he could pick oranges and figs. The old man would have liked to have a few more tasty treats on his table, or a new rug in his bedroom but, by and large, he was content and happy with his lot.

One day when he was fishing, he noticed a beautiful rainbow in the sky. As his eyes followed the graceful curve of the rainbow's arch, he was astonished to see it ended in the very stream where he was sitting! He scrambled over the bank and saw a small, clear rock lying in the water. The light from the rainbow fell on the glassy rock like spangles on a circus performer's costume – every colour and hue shone brightly: cerise pink, brilliant jade green, and turquoise blue brighter than the sea. The old man lifted up the rock in amazement. If only he had something this beautiful to give to his wife! But a poor man like him could never buy such riches. Feeling sorry for himself, a single tear slid down his cheek and landed on the rock.

"Aagh!" The old man gasped in shock. There on the rock, unmistakeably, lay a single diamond, its pure, shimmering colours sparkling in the sunlight. Trembling, his fingers uncurled and closed around the jewel. Incredibly, the rock had transformed his tear into a precious diamond! Suddenly he realised – if he could just make himself cry, he could become wonderfully rich. Carefully, he carried the rock home. Now all he had to do was cry!

At first, it was easy. He shut his fingers in the door… Ouch! And when his tears landed on the rock they turned into gleaming diamonds. He was thrilled! Now he could buy that new rug. Next, he read a sad story about a dog called Lassie. Once again, his tears fell on to the rock and became precious gems. Hurrah! Chocolate cake for supper! As time went by, he was able to do more things to make himself cry, so soon he was very rich indeed.

But now the old man was becoming greedy. He wanted more…but he was running out of ideas to make him cry. "I know!" he thought, "I'll sell my cat. That'll make me sad." The cat didn't want to be sold. He mewed and struggled as a lady carried him off to be her new pet. It was very sad and the old man cried a lot. This made dozens of diamonds, so he could afford a grand cat statue made of pure gold. How beautiful! Then he had another idea. "I'll tell the puppy she has to leave. That'll make me sad." Well, the puppy was horrified! She loved the old man! But he insisted, and as the poor little dog whimpered as she stumbled off into the distance, the old man's tears fell like rain. Now there were hundreds of diamonds! He could buy a beautiful silver ring with dogs engraved on it. How marvellous!

Now his house was like a palace, filled with all he could ever want. But still he wanted more. How could he make himself cry for the last time? Suddenly, he had a plan. "Dear wife," he said, "I must ask you to go and live far away. That will make me cry." Well, his poor wife! She wept and sobbed as she walked away. The old man cried as if his heart would break…and made more diamonds! Now he was the richest man in the world! He could have anything!

But when he looked around him, he realised he didn't have to try to make himself cry any more. Now his wife and pets had gone, he was all alone. He was so sad, he cried all the time. He had all the money in the world, but no one to share it with, to enjoy all the things that used to make him happy or to care about him. What a price to pay! He had all the riches he had ever dreamed about but now he knew that would never ever make him a happy man. He had possessions – but without love, he had only sadness.

Reflection

Sometimes, we think we can only be happy if we have lots of money. We forget that we have riches which money cannot buy – good friends, a wonderful school and a loving family who cares about us.

Instead of trying to gain more possessions we should try to gain more friendship. Without people to share things with us, nothing is enjoyable. Some things are more important than money or possessions.

Links

The Fisherman and His Wife by The Brothers Grimm. The moral of this story is not to be greedy and to value what one already has.
The Selfish Giant by Oscar Wilde. A special child teaches a selfish giant about the value of love and friendship and what is important in life.
The Wonderful Story of Henry Sugar by Roald Dahl. A story to help children

understand that having money or material possessions isn't everything.
King Midas – A Greek Myth which illustrates how a golden touch doesn't bring happiness.

Bible links

Luke: 12:13-21 The Parable of the Rich Fool explains why we should not devote our lives to the accumulation of wealth like the rich man who stored up his riches rather than putting them to good use.

Quote

"You aren't wealthy until you have something money can't buy."
Garth Brooks, American country music artist (b. 1962)

Prayer

Lord,
We thank you for all that we have – safe homes, kind friends and loving families. We pray for all those children who live in fear, poverty and distress. May you comfort them and help us to appreciate how lucky we are. Amen.

You could also:
- Carry out a pocket money survey.
- Design a money facts worksheet – e.g. "If I get £2 pocket money a week, how long will it take me to save up for a DVD costing £18?"
- Homework activity: "If I had £5". Go shopping and collate all the things you could buy with £5. How much change will you receive?
- Think of some fund-raising activities that you could do to raise money for charity – a cake sale, bring-and-buy sale, a concert, a sponsored swim, etc.

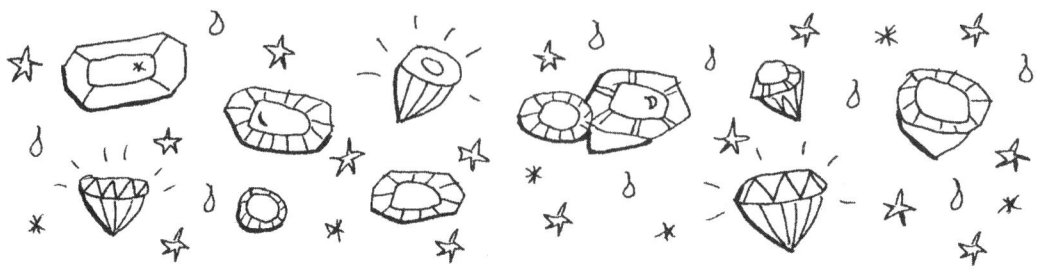

4. King Canute

> Taking responsibility

About one thousand years ago there lived a Viking king named King Canute. He was also known as Knud or even Knut – strange names for a king but not as odd as his father, 'Forkbeard', or his grandfather, 'King Gorm the Old', or even his great-grandfather, 'Harald Bluetooth'. All his people loved Canute. And what a sight he was! Tall and handsome (although they were too polite to point out his rather large, hooked nose), his hair was thick and wavy, and his eyes twinkled when he laughed. He wore a silver helmet topped with a dragon crest, a long red cloak fastened with a huge golden brooch, and boots richly embroidered in silk. He was powerful and important because he was the king, not just of England but of Denmark, Norway and some of Sweden, too. Everyone admired him enormously.

But, that was the problem. Because his people thought he was so marvellous, they believed King Canute could do everything. If they went fishing and didn't catch anything, they just shook their heads and said, "Never mind. King Canute can make the fish return. We'll just tell him." If the sun dried up all their crops they said, "Oh well. We'll ask the king to make it rain." And if foxes stole their chickens, they smiled and said, "Oh dear. We'd better ask King Canute to tell them not to eat our hens."

King Canute was exasperated. He knew he couldn't do everything the people expected. When the fishermen didn't catch anything, he wanted them to sail further out to sea where the fish were hiding and not expect him to conjure up a net of fish for them! When the farmers' crops shrivelled from lack of water, he wanted them to fetch buckets and water the plants themselves and not wait for him to magically make the rain fall! And when the foxes came to steal chickens, Canute wanted his people to bang pots to scare them and not imagine that he could ask them to keep away!

But every time the king tried to tell his people that they should do these things themselves, they didn't listen. They just smiled and said, "Oh, great and wondrous king! You are the most powerful person in this land! You can do whatever you wish. We are too weak to make a difference. That's why we leave everything to you."

King Canute realised that if his people didn't start to take responsibility, they would soon be in trouble. They would have no fish, no crops and no food. So, he decided to teach them a lesson. He dragged his enormous throne out to the beach and plonked himself down in it. Then he asked, "Do you think I am the most powerful man in this land?" His people quickly answered, "Oh yes, your majesty!" "Well," Canute continued, "you must think I can easily command the waves to stop!" "Yes! Yes!" they chorused. So Canute lifted up his hand and in a loud voice he boomed at the waves: "STOP RIGHT THERE!"

But the waves didn't stop. They kept on coming and coming until they reached his knees. His people were puzzled. What was happening? "STOP!" he roared again. But the waves didn't stop. They kept on coming until they lapped his neck. "STOP!" he gasped as his head disappeared. His people were horrified. They rushed down and dragged him out of danger. As they breathlessly pulled him to safety, soaking wet and covered in seaweed, they were surprised to see Canute was actually smiling. "Don't you see?" he told them, "I can't do everything. I'm just like you. You helped me when I needed you. You can be just as powerful as I am…when you try. Go home and be responsible for yourselves. I can't always be there to do things for you. And when you do something on your own, you'll feel so proud."

Reflection

Just like Canute's people, it seems easier and safer to let others take responsibility for us. We might feel it's too hard to organise our books or sort out our own possessions, to start our homework or fetch some food and drink. Often we wait for someone else to tell us what to do or how to do it. But see how proud you'll feel when you manage to do something all on your own. There's no such word as 'CAN'T'… it's spelled T… R… Y… 'TRY'.

Set yourself a goal each week. Think of things that someone else always does for you – get your uniform ready, make a snack, tidy your room, feed a pet. Can you take on that responsibility? Think of jobs in the classroom or playground and have monitor rotas – tidying the books, picking up litter, being a buddy for younger or lonely children. Report back to your class each week.

Links

Alfie Gives a Hand by Shirley Hughes. Alfie overcomes his shyness and becomes the most helpful guest at his first party without Mum.
Swiss Family Robinson by Johann David Wyss. The shipwrecked family become close as they bond over the experience of learning how to survive

as they face the formidable challenges of island life.
The Illustrated Mum by Jacqueline Wilson. Dolphin loves her disfunctional mother but she has to take on the huge responsibility of family carer as her mother's behaviour is so erratic.
Lola Rose by Jacqueline Wilson. Jayni/Lola Rose cares for herself and her vulnerable brother whilst their mother is treated in hospital.

Bible links

Jonah 1-4 The story of Jonah, who tried to avoid responsibility when God asked him to help.

Quote

"Time and tide waits for no man."
English proverb

Prayer

Dear God,
Give me strength to accept the things I can't change
And courage to change the things I can.
Help me to take responsibility and not rely on others.
I know you are always there to guide me.
Please help me to be strong.
Amen.

You could also:
- Make a rota for class monitor jobs.
- Consider how to take responsibility for wild animals. Make bird food balls, for example. What else could be done?
- Set up recycling stations in school – for paper, bags, plastic, etc. Organise a clothes collection point for charity donations.
- Set up a reading buddy scheme, where older children become reading partners with younger ones.

5. The Big Lion and the Little Rabbit

Stand up to bullies

Note: *This story is part of the Panchatantra, which was written over two thousand years ago. It is a collection of 87 stories about animals. These stories are told and acted out all over India.*

Once upon a time, in India, there lived a big lion in a jungle. He was absolutely ENORMOUS, with a shaggy, golden mane and smooth, sleek fur. His teeth were like glittering razors, glinting in the hot, bright sun. All the other creatures were afraid of him. Well, who wouldn't be? They knew that he could swallow most of them whole in one gulp…and still feel peckish. All day long, he prowled around the jungle searching for food, but as he had such an enormous appetite, he was never full up. So, he ate more and more of the poor animals.

"I am the king of the jungle!" he would roar in his deepest voice. "And I'm RAVENOUS! I need more food to fill my rumbly tummy."

Near the lion's den lived a community of rabbits. Before the lion arrived, they used to jump and play in the long grass, or chase butterflies. Now, they were too scared to go outside. They were terrified of the lion because they knew he loved rabbits – for breakfast, lunch and supper! They huddled together miserably in their burrows, until one day they decided to make an agreement with the lion. They told him:

"You can't be King if you keep eating all us animals. You won't have anyone left to rule over!"

The lion hadn't thought of that! He agreed it would be tricky to be a king if there was no one to boss around. The rabbits then told him their plan.

"You stay at home. We'll send one animal every day as food for you. Then you won't have to go hunting. But if we ever forget, you can come here and eat us all up!"

From then on, each day one animal was sent to the lion and the lion was pleased. This was like his very own Indian take-away!

The smallest rabbit had been watching with horror as the bullying lion scoffed all her friends one by one...but no one dared to stand up to him! The smallest rabbit didn't want to be a rabbit curry, and she knew she had to do something. She asked her friends to help, but they just sighed: "What can we do? We're only little. We can't make a difference against that big, bad bully. Sorry, but we can't help." They pretended not to notice as the brave little creature made her way determinedly towards the beastly lion. With no one else to stand up for them, she decided to be brave and think of a clever plan herself.

The lion was furious as he saw the tiny rabbit approaching his den. "GRRR! WHAT? That pathetic little creature is my lunch? She's not even big enough for a snack! Who's stolen the rest of my grub?"

The little rabbit pretended to be very afraid. She explained in a quiet voice: "The enormous lion has eaten all my friends, Mr Lion. I am all that's left."

The lion flew into a terrible rage. "Another lion? An ENORMOUS one? GRRR!" The little rabbit then explained that the massive lion had challenged him to a fight to see who was really the king of the jungle. The lion went purple with anger. "What a cheek! Take me to this ridiculous imposter!"

So, the rabbit led him to a deep well and told him that the other lion was in there. The lion peered in and saw his own reflection. He was livid! He thought it was the other lion so he let out a huge roar which echoed back at him. What? He dared to roar back? Furiously, he leapt into the well to attack the other lion.

Too late, he realised he had been tricked as he plunged into water…to be washed far away to the ocean. Hurrah! The little rabbit was overjoyed! She had stood up to the bullying lion and defeated him! So, she rushed home to spread the good news and celebrate with all her friends.

Reflection

This story shows us that however small we are we can still stand up to bullies. Think of ways you can stand up to bullies:
- Don't join in name-calling.
- Never hurt someone with your hands, feet or tongue.
- Be brave – even if you're the only one, stand up for what is right.
- Show others how to behave – always be kind and helpful, however rude and difficult someone is.
- If someone is being a bully, tell a grown-up. It's not telling tales – it's stopping bullying.

Links

St George and the Dragon: Brave George stands up to the dragon despite terrible risks.
James and the Giant Peach by Roald Dahl: James bravely escapes from the clutches of his wicked aunts.

Bible links

1 Samuel 17 The story of David and Goliath. Little David stands up to the big bully, Goliath

Quote

"Courage doesn't always roar. Sometimes courage is the quiet voice at the end of the day saying, 'I will try again tomorrow.'" Mary Anne Radmacher, American writer and artist

Prayer

Lord,
We know what is right.
We must not do wrong.
We should stand up for others
And always be strong.
Isaiah said: "If you follow God's rules, you will shine like a light for others to see."
Help me to shine, Lord.
Amen.

You could also:
- Appreciate people from other cultures. Use ICT to find facts about India (history, culture and festivals, geography).
- Consider corresponding with a school in India (see the British Council website, Global Gateway, at http://www.globalgateway.org.uk/).
- Hear more stories from the Panchatantra.
- Think about how to prevent bullying in the playground. Write rules to display, have playground 'buddies' and discuss in circle time.

6. Olga at Sports Day

> Pressures of consumerism; the importance of owning the 'right' labels; peer pressure

Olga was a very spoilt little girl. She had a pretty face but it was ruined because she always had a nasty frown and a sulky mouth. Whenever Olga wanted her own way she would lie on the floor and drum her heels on the ground and scream and scream, until her face went dark purple and the tip of her nose turned white with rage. I'm sorry to say, her mum and dad just gave in to this behaviour and let her have whatever she wanted. The result was, Olga was a very horrible little girl.

As her parents always bought her whatever she demanded, Olga had all the most expensive brand and designer labels you could imagine. And didn't she show off! She was always telling the others: "Look at my outfit! It's pure silk! And my bag is from Milan – it cost a fortune! And these shoes – they're the same ones America's top model wears!"

She was very mean to anyone who didn't have the 'right' labels on their clothes. After all, she would only wear clothes that came from the 'best' shops…and of course, they cost loads of money. Olga didn't care whether her family could afford them. She knew she'd just throw another tantrum and scream and scream, until her face went dark purple and the tip of her nose turned white with rage, and her parents would give in. So, she was always unkind if she saw something from the 'wrong' shop: "Oh no! He's wearing a coat from the market! I wouldn't dream of wearing anything from the market!"

She pointed out all the symbols and laughed at them.
"That's cool."
"That's quite cool."
"Oh, you're not cool."
"Look at that! Your trainers are so cheap I'm surprised the sole has stayed on!"

She was so horrible that she even teased children about what was in their lunch-box! If a biscuit had a plain wrapper on it, she called it 'cheap'. She didn't care if it was tastier than her fancy version. In fact, no matter what you had – bags, clothes, shoes, homes, TV… you name it – Olga laughed and mocked. She thought she had good taste because she spent so much money.

Worst of all, Olga always tried to encourage other people to join in with her sneering and teasing. Some people admired all her lovely possessions and they were a bit afraid of annoying her in case she teased them instead, so they didn't dare stand up to her. It was very sad.

Olga always loved having the chance to show off her marvellous clothes. When Sports Day came, she dressed in her best outfit and her nicest sandals to make all the other children jealous. She really enjoyed walking around hearing everyone gasp with amazement. How she laughed at the others who were wearing ordinary old trainers! Or plain shorts! Why, she had on her long, straight skirt from New York, and her high-heeled gold sandals with long sparkly laces. She smirked as she lined up for the obstacle race with the other children who were dressed so plainly. She'd show them how to look cool! Everyone stood on the starting line: 3, 2, 1…they're off!

Well, how the crowd roared…with laughter! Olga could hardly even walk in her tight skirt; she was waddling along like a duck! She couldn't even lift up her leg to jump over the bar so she had to clamber over it head first. When she got to a patch of slimy mud, her sandals had no grip so she skidded, flew up into the air…and landed on her bottom with a splat! The other children raced to the finishing line easily as they were dressed sensibly, but Olga took ages to stagger round the course. When she finally came in last in her muddy, useless clothes, she was really ashamed. How silly she looked now – even though all her things did have 'cool' labels.

Reflection

It doesn't matter about having the latest fashions or the top new toy. Sometimes, we worry too much about the right labels or symbols. Just because something costs lots of money doesn't mean it's good. We shouldn't tease others because they don't own something.

In some countries, children are so poor they only own the clothes they are wearing – and nothing else. Close your eyes and imagine you are a child like that, maybe living in the street, cold, hungry and afraid. How grateful you would feel if you just had a pair of shoes! Now think about your possessions. Do you own anything you no longer need? Could you give that to a charity to help others? That would make you feel good, and help someone worse off than yourself.

Links

Charlie and the Chocolate Factory by Roald Dahl: Spoilt, greedy children

see the error of their ways in Willy Wonka's factory whilst well-behaved Charlie is rewarded.
Cinderella's ugly sisters: despite the two ugly sisters' indulgent, extravagant tastes in expensive gowns and tickets to the ball, Prince Charming falls for Cinderella's charms rather than these unpleasant characters.

Bible links

John 8:12 Jesus is the light of the world. This symbol reminds us that Jesus makes us feel safe, shows us the way and helps us to see clearly.

Quote

"As we can't always get what we like, let us like what we get."
Spanish proverb

Prayer

Dear Lord,
You have given us many symbols to remind us how to live like you.
Help us to always be kind to people, just as you were kind to those who had no money, no food and no friends.
You are the Light of the World
And we follow as you guide us.
Amen.

You could also:
- Design an obstacle course in P.E.
- Find other symbols important to Christians (a cross, a fish, etc.)
- Design a clay shoe. Provide a variety of shoes to copy. Trainers are easiest; make two thumb pots and join together; keep the top of the shoe open. Fashion a shoe shape and decorate with "stitching", laces, etc. Glaze to finish.

7. Santa in a Muddle

> Coping with changes

It was the beginning of December and Father Christmas was very worried. All his reindeer were off sick with flu and most of his elves were still on holiday in Barbados, so he had lots to do. Rudolf realised how busy Santa was, so he decided to help. Being a very clever reindeer, he logged on to his computer and ordered a few surprises. Then, he sat back and waited for Christmas Eve, when he was sure the Big Man would be delighted with all the changes he'd arranged.

Oh dear! Santa wasn't happy at all. He was quite used to the way he handled Christmas every year. He knew the children would post letters to him early in December, then he would reply to each one. That would take a fortnight, then it took another day to stick the stamps on the envelopes and, finally, a week for the post to be delivered. But not this year.

This year, Rudolf had arranged for the children to e-mail their lists to Santa. The Big Man was horrified. He had never even turned a computer on before, let alone opened a million e-mails. He pressed a switch. "BLEEP!" The screen went black. He tried pressing the space bar. "BURP! BURP!" Now the computer started to make a terrible grinding noise. Father Christmas began to lose patience. He pressed 'Escape' six times in a furious rage. "BANG!" Oh dear.

Next, Santa went outside to load his sleigh. To his surprise, there were no reindeer patiently waiting, but instead there was a solar-powered space rocket. The Big Man was horrified. Who was going to show him how to work this machine? He was used to saying "Gee up!" and the reindeer would obediently trot off. He tried pressing the big red button marked "FIRE!" He took off like a cheetah on roller skates. "WHIZZZ!" Within six seconds he'd lapped the world twice and his sack had dropped off the back somewhere over Uzbekistan. Oh dear.

Finally, Santa went to find his atlas which guided him to the children's homes. Instead, there was a Satellite Navigation System – a sat nav – to show him the way. The Big Man was appalled. He'd never even used a mobile before, never mind a sat nav. He punched in BATH, ENGLAND for his first address. "Do you mean shower?" asked the tinny voice. "No!" Father Christmas shouted. "It's a town!" "A frown?" asked the tinny voice. "Are you sad?" Oh dear.

Poor Father Christmas was sad. He didn't like the idea of changing to this new technology. He was happy with everything the way it was. He was afraid of using things he didn't know much about. And everyone else knew what to do – it was just him who was left behind and looking rather silly. Why couldn't Christmas stay the same?

Suddenly, Rudolf appeared. "I'll help you!" he cried. "Trust me! I'll show you how to use all the new equipment then you can learn, too!" He showed Santa how to reply to all the e-mails at once – and all one million children received a reply immediately. He demonstrated how to fly the space rocket – so all the presents were delivered within an hour. And he programmed the sat nav so Santa never got lost once.

By midnight on Christmas Eve, Santa was back at home with Rudolf. For once, the two of them could relax and watch TV together before bedtime. "I'm so glad you helped me to change!" said Father Christmas. "All these new ideas seemed scary before, but once I calmed down and you offered to help, it wasn't half as bad as I thought it would be. Christmas has been much better this year!"

Rudolf smiled. He wasn't complaining. After all, this year he could put his hooves up and enjoy the Queen's Speech for the first time ever!

Reflection

We are often afraid when things change. We may be changing to a new school or class. Perhaps something in our family is about to change, like a new brother or sister, or a new step-parent, arriving. Moving to a new house or a different area can be scary. Or one of our friends may be saying goodbye.

At times like these, we must remember that everything else stays the same. We still have our old friends to help us and to be kind to us. Our families have many people who love and care for us. And we can always look forward to the new and exciting things that change will bring.

Don't forget, when someone we know has to deal with changes in their life, they may be scared or worried or lonely. We can help them by teaching them what we know and by always being there for them when they are finding it hard to be calm.

Links

A Little Princess by Frances Hodgson Burnett. When little rich girl Sara Crewe's father dies she is plunged into a world of poverty and starvation, yet she adapts admirably to the changes in her life with the help of her friends.
When Hitler Stole Pink Rabbit by Judith Kerr: a semi-autobiographical account of a young Jewish girl forced to flee the Nazis in the 1930s and cope with change in her strange new life as a refugee.

Quote

"If nothing ever changed, there'd be no butterflies in the world."
Anonymous

Bible link

Psalm 102:1-28 This prayer, from the Old Testament, was written a long time ago, but the sentiments never change – the man is asking God for help, telling Him he knows that whatever happens, God will always be the same, constant source of strength. This is as true today as it was then.

Prayer

Dear God,
Sometimes changes can seem frightening. We may be afraid when everything seems new and difficult.
Help us to remember that you will always stay the same, for ever by our sides to guide us and care for us.
Amen.

You could also:
- Write a 'handbook' of instructions to welcome a new pupil to your class.
- In an art lesson, see how colours change when mixed. Create the spectrum by using just primary colours.
- In a maths lesson, make price increases in a class shop – 'increase by 5p' or, for more advanced classes, 'increase by 10%'.
- Identify the changes in humans and animals as they grow; monitor, discuss and record.

8. Springtime – the joy of nature's creation

Creation myths; caring for our world;
the joy of spring

Note: *The Iroquois people are Native Americans who first settled in North America and Canada around 1,000 years ago. Like many people, they have marvelled at the amazing wonders of the Earth and they have a myth to explain its creation. They believed that a Great Creator made our world, and this story tells us how.*

Long ago, before the world was made, there was an island floating in the sky. Humans lived in this Sky World, and floating down below was a dark, watery place where animals, fish and birds lived. Sky Woman and her husband lived there happily. She was about to give birth to twins. She asked her husband to fetch a root from the Great Tree in the middle of the island. But, when he tugged at the roots he pulled up the whole tree and left a hole in the island.

Curious, Sky Woman peered through the hole to see the dark, swirling waters below. Suddenly, she slipped! Desperately, she clung to the roots twisted into the earth but, to her horror, the roots began to break and she ripped them from the ground. Screaming in terror, Sky Woman tumbled head-over-heels and began to plummet through the sky towards the deep, grey waters below.

Some birds – geese, doves and eagles – had watched, terrified for her, as she fell. Now they were determined to help the poor woman and her unborn babies. With their wings beating furiously, they flew in desperation towards Sky Woman. Swooping below her, they spread their wings out as wide as they could, and were filled with relief when she landed with a soft thud on their backs.

Watching far below was a great turtle and some small muskrats. "Quick!" cried the muskrats. "We must try to save this poor woman, too!" The turtle looked up anxiously and positioned himself directly beneath Sky Woman, who was gliding gently to the dark, watery place on the wings of the birds. "What can we do?" cried the little muskrats. "We're just too tiny to help!" Suddenly, the smallest muskrat had a brilliant idea. She dived down deep into the murky waters for a few minutes. When she reappeared, she was clutching a lump of soft, sticky mud between her paws. As quickly as a bolt of lightning, she spread the mud on the turtle's back and dived down for some more. "Hurry!" cried the turtle. "Copy your friend, then

Sky Woman will have somewhere soft to land!" With all the little creatures working so hard, a great pile of mud was soon spread across Turtle's back…just as Sky Woman landed gently. She was filled with joy and gratitude for the help the animals had given her, and she promised she would always take great care of all living things.

Gradually, the mud on the turtle's back spread until it became North America. Sky Woman planted the roots from the Sky Tree there and they grew food – corn, beans and strawberries. She sprinkled dust into the air and created stars. Then she made the Moon and the Sun.

Later she gave birth to her twin sons. One was called Sapling. He was kind and gentle. The other was called Flint and he was cold and hard. Sapling created what is good. He made animals that are useful to humans and plants that they could eat. He made the soft rain and the warm breeze.

But Flint destroyed much of Sapling's work. He put bones into fish and thorns on berry bushes. He stirred up violent hurricanes and tornados. He created winter, but Sapling gave it life so it could move to let spring come. Eventually, Sapling forced his brother to go away to live underground. Sometimes when Flint is angry, we see his power. That is a volcano.

The Iroquois people have great respect for birds and animals. Without the creatures' help, Sky Woman would have sunk to the bottom of the sea and the Earth would not have been created.

Reflection

Spring is a time when we look around and notice how beautiful our world is. We see baby animals playing in green fields, buds appearing on trees and new life everywhere. But we have a job to do to keep our world looking so fresh and lush. Let's think about how well we care for our local area.
- When you see litter, do you pick it up?
- Do you make lots of noise and disturb your neighbours?
- Do you recycle things like paper, cardboard and plastic bottles?

We are lucky to live in such a beautiful world, but we mustn't take it for granted – we should all take care of the place we live in.

Links

Creation myths from other cultures and times: Aborigine, Egyptian, Indian, Chinese, etc.

Bible link

Genesis 1:1–2:3 The Christian story telling how God created the world in six days and on the seventh he rested.

Quote

"Spring is nature's way of saying: 'Let's party!'" Robin Williams, American actor (b.1951)

Prayer

Dear God,
Thank you for all the wonderful life we see around us.
Thank you for newborn animals and buds on the trees.
Thank you for all the good things we have to eat.
Thank you God for making our world. Amen.

You could also:
- Design a poster encouraging everyone to take care of their environment (turning off lights, recycling, cleaning litter up).
- Make a zigzag book to illustrate the Creation story.
- Plant cress seeds in different conditions (no light/water/warmth/space/air) to establish the conditions seeds need to grow and thrive.

9. Harvest

> A time to work hard, share, think of others and
> be thankful for what we have

You might like to organise a class performance. You will need:
- Card head circlets with pipe-cleaners for antennae and black clothes (ants) or green clothes (grasshoppers)
- Seven cards with the letters: H A R V E S T
- Props, for example, deckchair, sunglasses, book, computer game, dusters, etc.

Some children could hold up the letters HARVEST, narrate the stories or read the prayers. Others could be ants, acting as directed. The grasshopper dances to the Grasshopper's Cumbia; other children could join in as the grasshopper's friends. The ants can march like soldiers when performing their chant.

Note: prepare individual cards for holding up to spell 'HARVEST'. Ask seven children to hold up the cards then ask them to change around as different words are spelled out.

HARVEST. This is a time to celebrate what we have. Some people do not have enough food, so they may **STARVE**. We are lucky to live in a country where we have enough to **EAT**. Let us remember others and **SHARE** our harvest with the poor.

Harvest is a time to give thanks for all the good things we have. We are very lucky because we have good food, safe homes and loving families. But there are many people in the world who do not have enough to eat. We should try to share what we have and to help others.

This is a story about someone who was lazy and did not want to help. It is called The Ants and the Grasshopper. It was written by a great storyteller called Aesop, a Greek slave who lived about 600 BC.

Once upon a time, there lived a community of ants. There were hundreds and hundreds of them – big ants, little ants, short ants, tall ants, puny ants with no muscles and enormous, strong ants with rippling biceps. There were black ones and red ones, young and old, male and female…in fact, every size, shape and type of ant you could ever imagine. They didn't notice any of the differences between themselves because they all worked together for the whole community. And how hard they worked! They were always busy, racing around, rushing about. Hurry, hurry, no time to stop. At harvest time, they worked especially hard to make sure they had enough food to keep in their store cupboards so they would have plenty to eat during the cold winter months. They worked busily without a break, from sunrise to sunset. They hardly stopped at all.

They raced around collecting fruit and vegetables to prepare and store over the winter. They ground the grain to make flour. They dusted and cleaned their cupboards. They helped their neighbours and friends so they could all enjoy a comfortable winter. To keep their spirits up, they sang chants as they marched and worked.

Note: *Play 'The Harvest Song'.*

Meanwhile, their neighbour, the grasshopper, was far more relaxed.
He laid in the sun… He read a book… He had a long snooze… He played computer games… In fact, he did anything but work! Best of all, the grasshopper loved to dance and sing… How he laughed when he saw the ants working so hard! But not once did he collect food at harvest time, to prepare for the winter.

Note: *Act this part out, playing 'The Grasshopper's Cumbia' when the grasshopper dances.*

Then, winter came. Fat, cold snowflakes twirled down to the ground and the world turned white and harsh. The trees were bare as the leaves fell and the berries disappeared. No matter how hard you searched, you couldn't find a grain of wheat or piece of fruit to pick. The ground was hard and icy, and it was impossible to dig in search of a few vegetables. The grasshopper was desperate. He was cold and miserable and he had no food to eat.

He looked inside all his jars and tins, but they were empty. He checked inside all his cupboards but they were bare. He even searched under his bed, hoping to find just a few crumbs of food, but there was nothing there at all. Shivering with cold and hunger, he went to ask the ants if they would share their food.

"You should have worked like us. Now you are hungry. You laughed at us for being busy, but who's laughing now?"

Reflection

This story shows that we should always be ready to work hard and prepare for the future. We should help when we can. And we must always try to share. Perhaps you can think of a way to donate your old toys to charity, or collect dried goods to give to elderly people in your area. And remember those people who live in countries where they never have enough food to eat and hunger is a way of life.

Links

Mr Busy by Roger Hargreaves. Mr Busy can't sit still and do nothing: he is always busily rushing around, in contrast to his placid neighbour Mr Slow who has a lie-in on the morning of their picnic.
The Tale of Mrs Tittlemouse by Beatrix Potter. Mrs Tittlemouse is a terribly tidy little wood mouse who despairs as messy visitors make extra work for her.

Bible link

Luke 6:38. Share what you have with others and you shall be rewarded. The measure you give will be the measure you receive.

Quote

"Striving for success without hard work is like trying to harvest where you haven't planted." David Bly, American educator and legislator (b.1952)

Prayer

Dear God,
Thank you for all the wonderful food we have to eat,
Which comes from all over the world.
Help us to take care of the land
And not waste what we have.
We will remember those who are hungry
And share what we have with everyone.   Amen.

You could also:
- Collect food labels then use a map to identify where our food comes from.
- Calculate the air miles of our food using an atlas.
- Write your own harvest prayers of thanksgiving.
- Write a harvest acrostic poem.

10. Differences

> Be tolerant, don't judge by appearances, embrace differences, don't prejudge others

Once upon a time, there lived three animals – a pig, a goat and a sheep. They were great friends, always laughing and sharing jokes. They all liked doing the same kind of things: they read the same books, played the same games and ate the same kind of food.

One day, a new animal arrived. Everyone was horrified – it was a ferret! They knew all about ferrets, even though they'd never met one before!

"Ferrets are filthy!"
"Ferrets are fierce!"
"Ferrets have fleas!"
"Everyone knows – you can't trust a ferret at all!"

When they saw the ferret unpacking all the things for her new home, they felt sure they had been right. It was so messy! There were two enormous dustbins filled to the brim with rubbish, and the whole place was littered with strange jars of peculiar foods. The goat went to see for himself. When he got closer, he smelled a delicious smell as the ferret was cooking supper. He watched as she carefully scrubbed and washed the vegetables until they were gleaming. The goat was impressed. He rushed home to tell the others that, actually, the ferret seemed to be a clean, careful type of creature.

"No, no! Remember! Ferrets are filthy!"
"Ferrets are fierce!"
"Ferrets have fleas!"
"Everyone knows - you can't trust a ferret at all!"

So the sheep went to look. He was certain the ferret would be a lazy layabout who would lounge around all day doing nothing but stealing their food. To his surprise he saw she was very busy! She had lots of tools which she was using to make a delightful home. She was hammering, cutting, chopping and banging away. The little house was beautifully made from the finest wood. The sheep rushed back to tell the others that, actually, the ferret seemed to be a hard-working, busy creature.

> "No, no! Remember! Ferrets are filthy!"
> "Ferrets are fierce!"
> "Ferrets have fleas!"
> "Everyone knows – you can't trust a ferret at all!"

The animals felt sure they were right not to trust the ferret, so they decided to ignore her. Why, they knew what she was like! They wouldn't be friends with her sort. They agreed she was different from them. She wasn't from around here. Everyone knew how horrible ferrets were. They would have nothing to do with her. After all, she was a filthy, fierce, untrustworthy animal.

Then, one day, the pig's old enemy the Big Bad Wolf came round to pay him a visit. Uh oh! Being a big, bad bully, Wolfie couldn't resist being nasty. Taking a huge deep breath, he filled his lungs with air…then…PHHHOAAR! He huffed and he puffed and blew most of pig's house down! The animals were terrified. They ran around helplessly, shrieking: "Help! Save us!" When the ferret heard the commotion, she was horrified. How dare Wolfie treat those poor animals like that! Fearlessly, she swung into action. "GERONIMO!"

She ran up behind Wolfie with two dustbin lids and shouted "AIM…FIRE!" When she crashed the lids together, the wolf leapt into the air as though his tail was on fire! He thought the farmer had shot him with his gun! He raced off faster than a squirrel on a skateboard. Once he'd disappeared, the ferret fetched her tools and began to repair the house. In no time at all, pig's home was mended and good as new.

The goat, the pig and the sheep hung their heads in shame. Whilst they were panicking, the ferret had saved them! They realised that although the ferret was different from them, she was also braver and cleverer than all of them put together. Now they knew all about ferrets.

> "Ferrets are fabulous!"
> "Ferrets are fun!"
> "Ferrets are faithful friends!"

Reflection

Sometimes we don't like people for all sorts of silly reasons – just because they come from a different place or they look or dress differently from us. How boring the world would be if we were all the same!

Think about your best friend. How are you different? Do you have the same colour eyes, the same hairstyle and the same skin tone? These things don't matter. What matters is that they're kind, generous and friendly. That's why you chose them to be your friend.

Links

Something Else by Kathryn Cave. 'Something Else' is different from all the other creatures. He feels like an outcast until he meets 'Something' and they form a friendship based on their differences.
The Ugly Duckling by Hans Christian Andersen. Everyone is unkind to the Ugly Duckling because he looks so different.
Children Just Like Me by Barnabas and Anabel Kindersley. A beautifully photographed reference book illustrating some of the similarities and differences between children from a variety of cultures around the world.

Bible link

Mark 1:40 Jesus heals the leper. Jesus cared for everyone, despite their appearance or health or wealth.

Quote

Never judge a book by its cover. Proverb

Prayer

Dear God,
Many people see you in different ways. They love and serve you in different ways, too.
We all see things in different ways. Otherwise, we would all be the same.
Help us to enjoy sharing our differences with each other.
Help us to enjoy all the many different things in our world. Amen.

You could also:
- Paint self portraits, mixing your own flesh tones (no one is the same). Display these around a title: "We are all different".
- Compare and contrast life for children in a different part of the country or world. What things are different? What are the same? Play 'Find the Difference' games. Spot the difference between two pictures – see http://www.spotthedifference.com/explorer.asp for examples.

11. Mother's Day

> Our mothers are special

Felipe was a thoughtless, lazy boy. If you went to his house, you'd think there was a lump of lard dressed in school uniform sitting on the sofa. All he ever did was watch TV or play on his games console. In fact, as he sat scoffing crisps and lazing around all day, he found it very difficult to do very much at all, except change the channels on the remote and yell "MUM!" whenever his glass of cola needed refilling.

He never did a thing his mother asked. Every day he would lollop in from school, straight into the living room without bothering to take off his trainers. There would be mud all over the carpet and his mother would despair. "Please take your shoes off," she would ask him. "It's one of the few things I ask you to do."

But Felipe didn't care. Why should he have to stop for a minute to untie his laces and find a space to fit his trainers into the cupboard? Anyway, he'd be out again in a few minutes so it wouldn't be worth it. So his poor mother had to fetch the dustpan and brush and sweep up the mud, then drag out the heavy vacuum cleaner and clean the carpet again.

When Felipe had a snack, he didn't do as his mother asked either. He'd just take the bread out of the cupboard, lay it on the worktops without a plate so crumbs fell everywhere, then he'd smear butter all over the sink and drip jam on the floor. When his mother saw the mess she'd despair. "Please tidy up after yourself," she would ask him. "It's one of the few things I ask you to do."

But Felipe didn't care. Why should he have to waste his precious time cleaning up the kitchen when his mother was going to make it all messy again when she made lunch? He didn't care if it attracted flies or if jam got stuck to the dog's paws. He'd be in the other room watching TV by then. So his poor mother had to fetch the dishcloth and the cleaning spray and polish the sink and wipe up the crumbs and scrub the dog's paws until all the mess was cleared up again.

When Felipe had a bath he never bothered to follow his mother's rules in the bathroom either. He'd run all the taps and use up all the hot water, then he'd tip loads of his mother's favourite bubble bath in to make lots of bubbles – which

37

always ended up spreading across the floor making it slippery. Then he'd get out and leave a dirty, muddy ring around the sides of the bath tub and fling his wet towel on to the bed. When his mother saw the state of the bathroom she'd despair. "Please clean the bathroom," she'd say. "It's one of the few things I ask you to do."

But Felipe didn't care. He was far too busy to hang around cleaning up a few drops of water. And what did he care if the dog went skidding across the slippery floor and landed in the toilet? So his poor mother had to pick up the towel and sponge the bath tub and mop the floor. She was exhausted.

Then she had an idea. "If Felipe can't see why he should follow my rules," she thought, "I'll just have to show him."

So on Saturday when Felipe woke up and came downstairs, there was no bacon and egg cooking as usual. "Where's my food?" he demanded in surprise. "You always cook me breakfast on Saturdays. It's one of the few things I ask you to do."

"Sorry Felipe," Mum explained, "but I just can't be bothered to follow your rules today."

At ten o'clock, Felipe stood by the car waiting for his mother to drive him to his swimming lesson. But instead she was reading the newspaper! "Mum, we always go swimming on a Saturday," cried Felipe. "It's one of the few things I ask you to do!"

"Sorry Felipe," said Mum, "but I want to read the newspaper today. I just haven't got the time to follow your rules."

At tea time, Felipe brought down his piggy bank so his mother could put in his pocket money.

"Sorry Felipe," Mum said, "But I don't want to give you any money. You'll only waste it."

Felipe was astonished. He was about to tell her it was one of the few things he asked her to do, but then he realised. If he never did as his mother asked, why should she have to do what he wanted? He felt very ashamed of himself. So, he rushed off to tidy the kitchen, the bathroom and the rest of the house. And now he knows why we should all do as our mothers ask – because they love and care for us, and they do so much to help us without asking for much in return.

Reflection

Think about your mother. What makes her special? Is it because she cooks delicious food, keeps the house tidy, helps with your homework or plays with you? Does she tell funny jokes? Does she sing like an angel? Does she dance round the house? Is she good at sport? A careful driver? A good listener?

We are glad we have such wonderful mothers who love us, no matter how difficult we are. Let's promise to be especially good to her on Mother's Day.

Links

The story from the Bible about the wisdom of King Solomon, choosing who was the real mother of a baby. (1 Kings 3:16-28)
The March of the Penguins. A National Geographic Film which shows that even in the harshest place on earth, a mother's love will flourish; a true story of how penguins raise their chicks in the face of enormous difficulties.

Bible link

Luke 1:46–55 (Magnificat) Mary's joy at being the mother of Jesus.

Quote

"Mothers hold their children's hands for a short while, but their hearts for ever." Author unknown

Prayer

Dear God,
All mothers are special
But my mum's the best.
Grant her health and happiness
And peace so she can rest.
She's busy doing things for me,
She works from dawn to dusk.
I'm glad that you take care of her;
I love her very much.
Thank you for all our mothers
But especially for mine.
Amen.

You could also:

- Write a recipe for a Perfect Mum. What do you need? (love, laughter, care) What don't you need? (smart clothes, fast car).
- Make a Mother's Day card.
- Design a Mother's Day gift voucher, e.g. "This is to certify that (name) is the best mum in the world. She is entitled to one hour of free washing up."

12. Tanabata – a Japanese Festival

> Work hard to achieve goals;
> loyalty; tenacity

In Japan, a very famous festival takes place every year on the seventh day of the seventh month. It is called Tanabata, and during this time you will see brightly coloured strips of paper hung from bamboo poles outside people's houses. This story tells us why.

The Emperor of the Sky was strong and powerful. He could do whatever he pleased, whenever he liked, as he ruled the heavens. He lived in a palace high in the clouds with his seven daughters. The youngest was a beautiful girl called Orihime. She was tall and slender with ebony eyes and long, flowing hair which framed her delicate face perfectly. She was a talented weaver, so her father was delighted as she could make materials from the finest silken threads in every colour of the rainbow. Every day she would sit at her loom looking down on the Earth below and weave these beautiful cloths, singing softly to herself.

But although she loved her father and their beautiful palace in the sky, Orihime was also very lonely. One day she went for a walk on the Earth and met a humble shepherd boy called Kengyu. Although he was very poor, he was kind and thoughtful, and he cared for Orihime very much. The young couple soon fell in love and were married. It was a marriage made in heaven as they were so much in love.

At first, the emperor was pleased to see his daughter so happy. But after a while, the pair began to neglect their jobs as they were so busy with each other. Orihime did not do her weaving and that made her father furious. He decided to separate the couple as a punishment, and send them far apart so the Moon and the stars were between them. To their horror, Orihime and Kengyu had to live on opposite sides of the Milky Way where they could never ever hope to see each other again.

Poor Orihime was so sad her tears fell like rain. She wept with grief at being parted from her true love. The emperor did not have a heart of stone so he took pity on her. "I promise," he said in a deep, rumbling voice, "that if you both work hard, I will allow you two to meet…but just for one day a year. If you care for each other as dearly as you claim, you will agree."

The young couple were delighted and they vowed that they would both try their hardest to please the emperor. They prayed that their wish to be together would come true, and they worked almost without stopping every day for a whole year. On the 7th July, a magpie appeared in the sky and its wings made a bridge across the Milky Way. Now Orihime and Kengyu could be together…but for just one day.

It is said that on that morning, there is often drizzle as Orihime weeps for her husband. During July, the stars Vega (which is Orihime) and Altair (which is Kengyu) are clearly seen in the sky, separated by the Milky Way.

In Japan, people write wishes on strips of coloured paper for the festival of Tanabata. They also make origami shapes from paper. They tie these to bamboo poles outside their homes. They often ask for help to work hard and to improve their skills – just as Orihime did.

Reflection

If we work hard and do our best, we can often achieve our dreams. We should also help others who are trying to work hard. We could:
- Help them if they are stuck.
- Try not to disturb them.
- Praise them for doing their best.
- Follow their lead.

Links

The Herdsman and the Weaver, a Korean folk tale. The sad story of the herdsman and the weaver who were allowed to see each other only once a year as punishment for not doing their work. This story reflects the sorrow of the separation of Koreans and also their hopes for reunion.
The Willow Pattern story. A romantic fable, with its Shakespearean overtones of doomed love and tragedy. This timeless tale of star-crossed lovers appeals to the imagination whilst the intricate Willow Pattern itself has been hugely popular for centuries. A young woman and her lover escape her cruel father, only to die tragically; their souls are immortalised as two doves in the pattern.
Romeo and Juliet by William Shakespeare. The children of two feuding families, Romeo of the Montague family and Juliet of the Capulet family, both love and die in the course of this play, one of Shakespeare's most famous tragedies.

Bible link

Parable of the Pearl (Matthew 13:45–46) Jesus told this story to show how it is worth every effort to belong to God's Kingdom.

Quote

"Nothing is impossible to the willing heart."
John Heywood, English poet and playwright (1497–c.1580)

Prayer

Lord,
Grant me the strength of eagles' wings to soar.
When things are tough, stay by my side and guide me on my way.
Help me to work hard and support others, just as you support me.
Amen.

You could also:
- Make a display of "Our wishes". Using washing-up liquid and paint, "bubble print" a cloud shape, then write out a desired wish and display in the classroom suspended from a fishing line.
- Paint scenes from the Willow Pattern story using blue paints or pens on paper plates
- Make origami shapes such as a dog ('inu'):
   1. Fold your square in half diagonally. Crease.
   2. Fold the triangle in half again, crease and open it back out.
   3. Turn the triangle so the long side is at the top. Fold down a corner to make an ear.
   4. Do the same to the other corner, ensuring the ears are even.
   5. Fold the bottom point up to form a nose.
   6. Draw the dog's face.
   See: http://www.en.origami-club.com/easy/dogface/dogface/index.html

13. Visitors from Outer Space

> Welcoming visitors; following school rules;
> being part of a caring community

We are all very proud of our school. We know we are polite, hard-working, sensible and thoughtful. We are always pleased to welcome visitors. But have you ever thought how visitors see us? Listen to this story.

It was (time/date). Earlier that week, two aliens had left their distant planet to visit Earth. They were a peculiar pair, with six ears dangling on springs from their knees, and their noses squeaked as they dragged along the ground behind them. Stranger still, they never chatted together or even smiled. They sat glumly, playing their own computer games which they controlled with their eyebrows. They didn't care that they were a million miles from home – after all, no one had bothered to wave them goodbye. They had no postcards to write because no one missed them at all.

The aliens felt quite excited as their rocket landed silently in the playground of (name of school) in (name of town). They wanted to write a report about everything they found so they could tell the others on their planet how these strange Earth people lived. As they wandered around the playground feeling rather lost, a young girl ran up to them. She smiled and held out her hand and said in a cheerful voice: "Welcome to (name of school). I'm so pleased to meet you. May I show you round?"

The first alien was so surprised he almost fell on to his chins. "How strange! This is not like our planet! On our planet, we just ignore visitors! They're too much trouble." The second alien wrote: "The children at (name of school) are warm and friendly to visitors. They show us hospitality."

The aliens hopped over to where two children were playing a game. They were having great fun – laughing and joking with each other. Suddenly, one of the children tripped and fell. Her friend helped her up and fetched a plaster. Then he stayed with her until she felt better.

The first alien was so surprised he almost fell on to his heads. "How strange! This is not like our planet! On our planet, we can't be bothered to look after people who fall over. We just walk away and find new friends." The second alien wrote: "The children of (school) care for others who are hurt, sad or lonely. They show compassion."

Next, they slithered up to six children playing a ball game together. It looked great fun – they were taking turns and sharing. Everyone was shrieking with laughter. They helped the smaller children who weren't good at catching and included everyone who wanted to play.

The first alien was so surprised he almost fell on to his tummy buttons. "How strange! This is not like our planet! On our planet, we don't like to share. We keep everything for ourselves." The second alien wrote: "The children of (name of school) play happily together. They share their things and include everyone in their games. They show community spirit."

Finally, they pressed their eyeballs against a classroom window and peered inside. They could see children working hard, all doing their best. They were reading books and writing neatly. They listened to others and disturbed no one.

The first alien was so surprised he almost fell on to his noses. "How strange! This is not like our planet! On our planet we are too lazy to work hard. We can't understand why we know nothing!" The second alien wrote: "The children of (name of school) work hard and follow the classroom rules. They always do their best."

When break ended, the children lined up sensibly and went inside. The aliens were very sad. They realised that their planet was not as happy as here. They had seen that the children really care about each other and that their school is a friendly, welcoming place where they learn lots, work hard and follow the rules. The aliens both agreed:

"What a wonderful visit! I wish we could stay for ever! Let's ask (name of headteacher) if they have two places for us."

Reflection

Remember always to show our visitors: HOSPITALITY, COMPASSION, COMMUNITY.
We should show them that we work hard and do our best.
Think about the 'Golden Rules' for our school.
Which three words would you like a visitor to describe you as?

Links

Town Mouse and the Country Mouse by Aesop. A contrast between life in the countryside and life in the town as each mouse takes care of his visiting cousin and discovers how visitors view the different lifestyles.
The Fox and the Stork by Aesop. Treat others how you expect to be treated. A stork is treated unkindly when she visits a fox so she returns the treatment when the fox pays her a visit.
Drop a pebble in the water. Poem by James Foley. Kindness (and unkindness) spreads like ripples from a pebble dropped into the water.
I'll take you to Mrs. Cole! by Nigel Gray. A heart-warming story of how a child is welcomed into a chaotic, untidy house with unexpected warmth and friendship.

Bible link

Luke 10:38-42. When Jesus visited Mary and Matha in Bethany, Mary sat and listened to him yet Martha was too busy. We should remember what is important and treat visitors with respect.

Quote

"Do right. Do your best. Treat others as you want to be treated."
Lou Holtz, retired American football coach (b. 1937)

Prayer

Dear Lord,
Help us to welcome all our guests with a warm greeting and friendly smile.
Show us how to treat others just as you treated visitors – with kindness, compassion and hospitality.
For everyone who arrives as a stranger, may they leave as our friend.
Amen.

You could also:
- Make a visitors' book with comments from all the visitors to your school.
- Make a tourists' information guide about your school. What are the best/prettiest/most interesting bits?
- Make a list of rules for the classroom and playground. Why are these rules necessary?

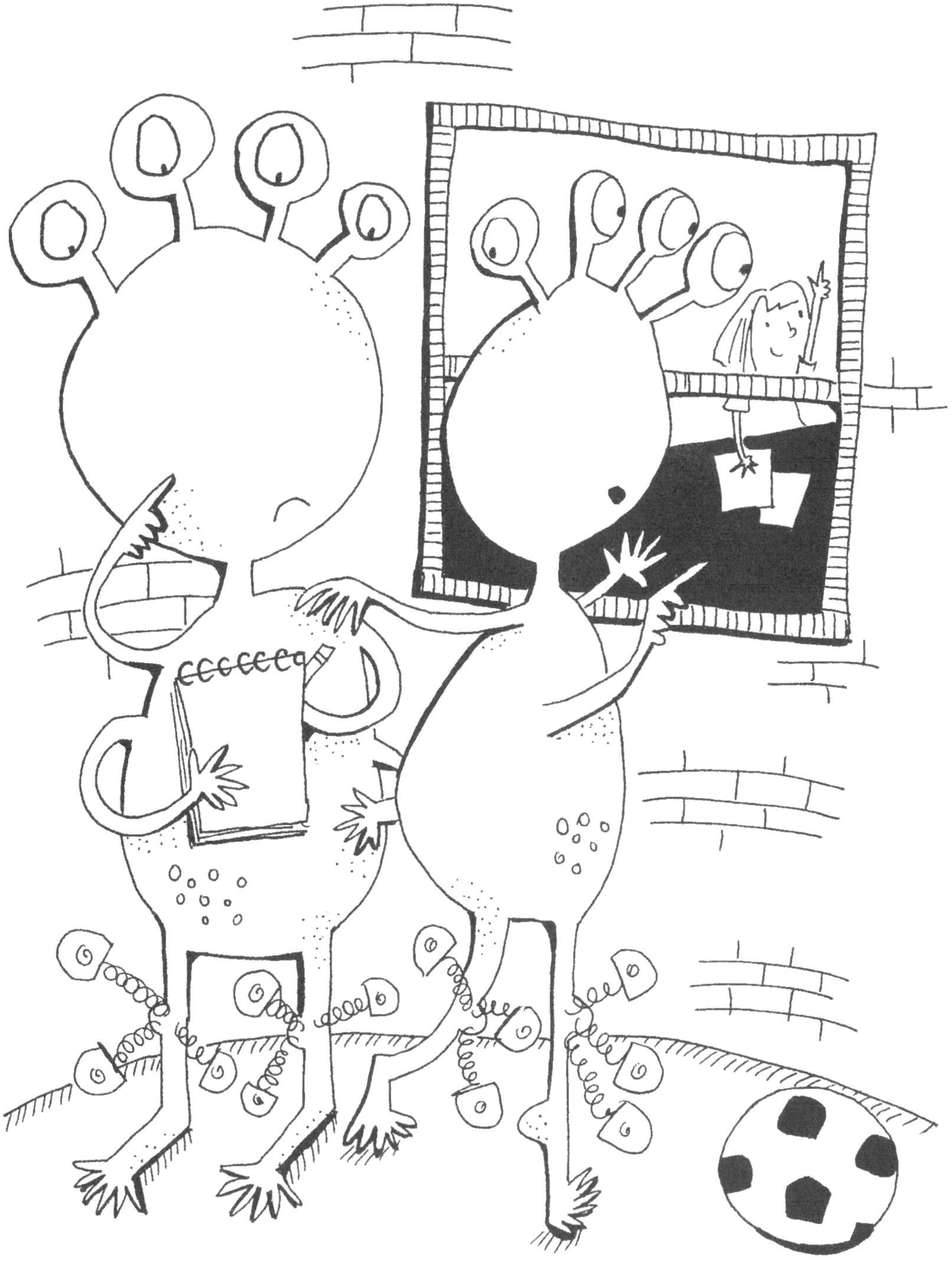

Other assembly books from Southgate:

For KS1:
First Steps – Stories for Assembly and PSE by Gordon Aspland
Starting Out – Stories for Assembly and PSE by Gordon Aspland
Magic Moments – Stories for Assembly and PSE by Christine Dawe

For KS2:
Choices – Stories for Assembly and PSE by Gordon Aspland
Consequences – Stories for Assembly and PSE by Gordon Aspland
Feelings – Stories for Assembly and PSE by Gordon Aspland
Situations – Stories for Assembly and PSE by Gordon Aspland